But...

...Church is *Boring*!

Bible study for young people
who don't like going to church.

Copyright © 2021 H. C. Dill & Peter Cross
(Reflections: M. McKinnell)

All rights reserved.

ISBN: 9798537834991

Introduction

T.V., internet, playing sport, catching up on homework, shopping... or even just lying in bed! There are a lot of things you could be doing on a Sunday morning. So, why go to church? Especially when church is... *boring!* The truth is... you don't *have* to go, not if you want to earn God's favour. God's promises to you are assured, whether you hit the pews* on a Sunday morning or not.

However, many Christians make the effort to go to church anyway. Why? Well, we're glad you asked...
In this book, we'll think about why Christians have gathered together in worship for centuries, and why they still do, even though it sometimes leads to persecution. Through Bible study and reflection, this book will help you to find your own motivation for joining with God's worldwide community. And, who knows? You may even uncover some strategies to make the whole experience a bit less... *boring!*

*Other seating options are available.

How to use this book

This book is divided into sections:
Prepare - is an opportunity to reflect on your starting point, either individually or in a group discussion.
Bible Study - time to dig deeper into God's word. You will need a Bible handy to complete this section.
Reflection - creative writing to lead you into prayer.
Going Deeper - offers ideas for personal prayer and reflection.
Ideas for Larger Youth Groups - suggests games, projects and ideas for youth leaders in a large group setting.
Ideas for All Age Worship - suggests ways in which young people could share their learning with God's people of all generations.

How to find a Bible Passage

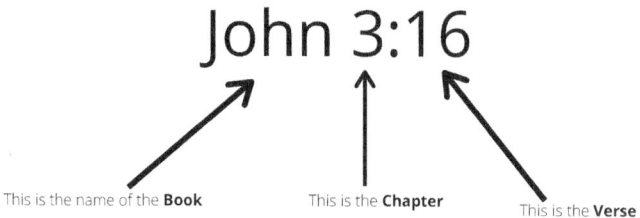

This is the name of the **Book** This is the **Chapter** This is the **Verse**

Go to the **Contents** page of your Bible and look up the name of the **book**. (Old Testament and New Testament books might be listed separately, or in alphabetical order instead of page order.)

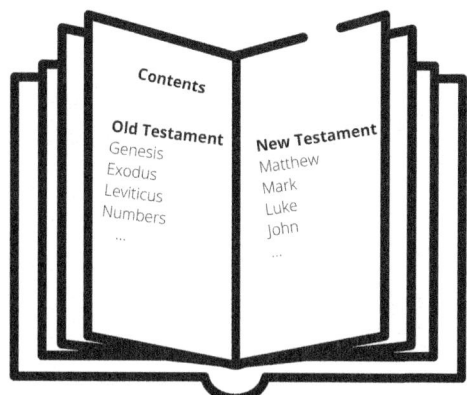

Within each book, the larger numbers at the head of each section are the **chapter** numbers, and the smaller ones within the text are the **verse** numbers.

Prepare

Here are some different types of church....

Which ones have you been to?

Are there any that you would like to try?

Choose a picture that best represents the church that you usually go to, or draw your own!

 *Church is...*

How would you finish this sentence?

Your Thoughts and Reflections.

Use this space to note down your responses to the 'prepare' questions, and any thoughts and feelings as you begin this study book.

Bible Study 1
by Peter Cross

**But...
...I can't be bothered!**

What should you not chuck in the bin?

Hebrews 10

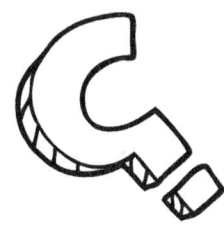

Look again at Hebrews 10:35
for the answer.

 It's Sunday...again. You've got to get up and go to church...again. Why do we have to keep going week after week?

Believe it or not, that's an excellent question! It opens up some really exciting ways to see worship and think about how we relate to God.

Before we get into it, why do you think we should go to church?

What are some of the reasons you have for not wanting to go to church?

The short answer is that we don't have to keep coming back week after week, actually. Nothing about going to church or showing up regularly makes God any happier or makes us any more "saved" than we were before. So why have Christians, since the beginning of the church almost 2000 years ago, continued to meet together regularly, if it wasn't to earn God's favour?

Let's turn to Hebrews. The letter is full of wisdom, but it can also be a bit challenging to understand. We don't really know exactly who wrote it. We have a few good guesses, but they never introduce themselves (like Paul always did). We do know that the writer knew a lot about Judaism (and was probably Jewish before becoming Christian), and that some of the logic they use would have made a lot of sense to the Jewish-Christian readers of their day... (but we're not as quick to make the same connections!)

The whole letter of Hebrews is all about how great Jesus is. In Hebrews, Jesus is greater than the angels, he's the great High Priest, and he's greater than the whole sacrificial system of the Old Testament. (That was when they all brought their grain, their cattle and sheep, and other things to give to God in the Temple in order to have their sins forgiven).

Your Notes

Compare verses 1-3 of Hebrews 10 with verse 10. What is the difference between the sacrifice of Jesus Christ and the sacrifices made under the law?

Under the law, day after day, week after week, month after month, and year after year they had to go and offer sacrifices. The greatest sacrifice of all came once a year, on the Day of Atonement, when the High Priest would sacrifice a lamb for the sins of all Israel. But he had to do it every year! Sin, Sacrifice, Rinse, Repeat. The author of Hebrews is arguing that the sacrificial system could never really work because it was a never-ending cycle... there was no way out! (10:1-4)

Are there some parts of church that feel like that to you? Why do you think they feel like that?

What was Jesus able to do, accoring to verse 14?

In verse 16, how are we able to know the right way to live, now that we are not under the law of the Old Testament?

Does this means that Christians will never do anything that is sinful or wrong?

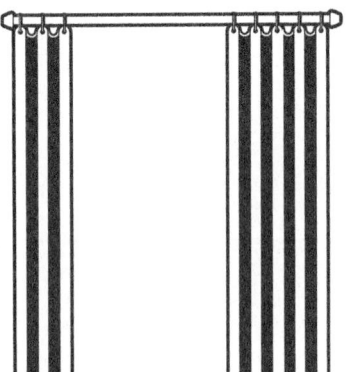

Look at verse 20. Remember in the story of Jesus' death how the curtain in the Temple was torn in two (Matthew 27:51)?

That meant that there is no longer anything standing in the way of us and God. No priests. No Sacrifices. No nothing.

Your Notes

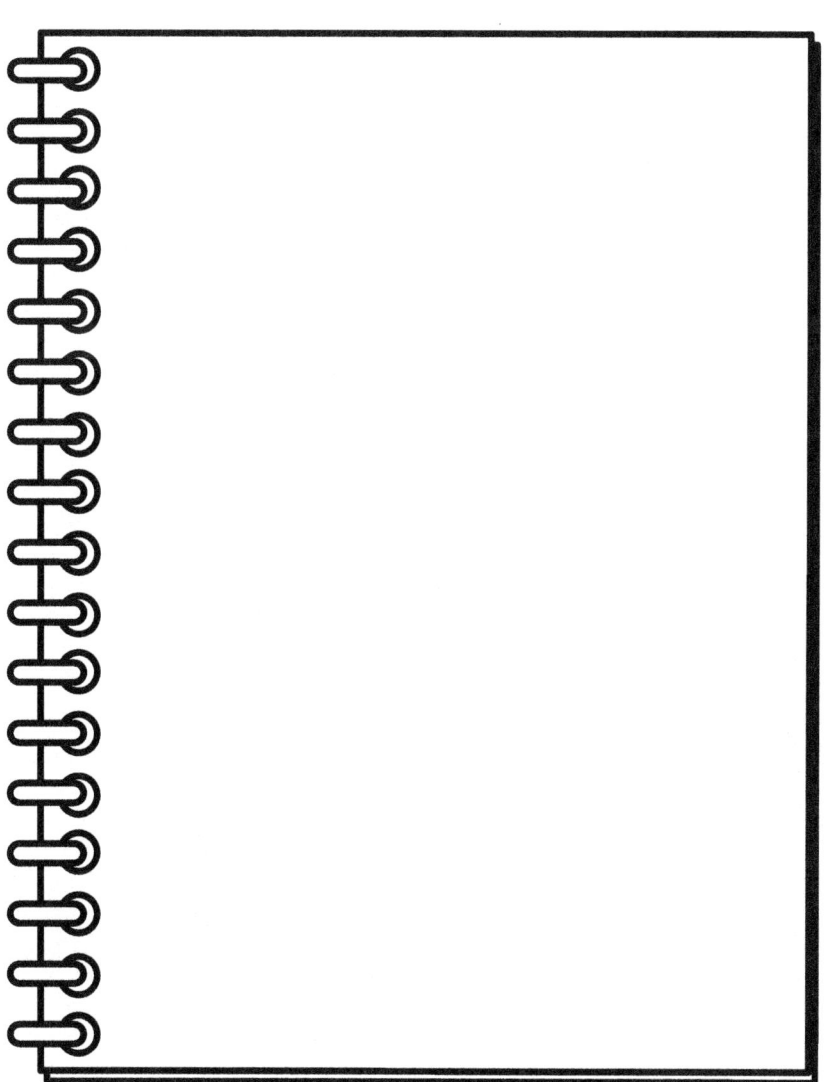

I said earlier that nothing about going to church week after week is what saves us. It doesn't! That endless cycle system is gone and done away with. We don't earn God's love by repeating acts over and over. Jesus was able to end that whole thing.

So, why do we still go to church?

Go back to the reasons for going to church that you wrote down at the start of this study. What do you think about those answers now that you have read some of Hebrews 10?

There are lots of reasons, some of which are just plain practical. It's nice to see friends. We help each other out. We learn things about God and Jesus. We celebrate things like Communion and Baptism together. We encourage one another. These are things that we can't really do by ourselves!

Some other reasons have to do with historical factors, like many people being unable to read or write or even have access to many books (or scrolls!) So, you had to meet together to tell and hear the stories! See? Practical!

What other practical reasons can you think of for meeting together regularly these days? Read verses 19-25 for some ideas.

Verses 26-31 have some pretty harsh words for those early Christians who may have turned their back on the community. But look at verses 30 and 31. Whose job is it to judge those who have turned away?

Looking at verses 32-39, (especially 33) can you think why some of the first believers might have deserted the church?

How are church-goers treated in your own peer group? Is it easy to have the confidence mentioned in verse 35?

Your Notes

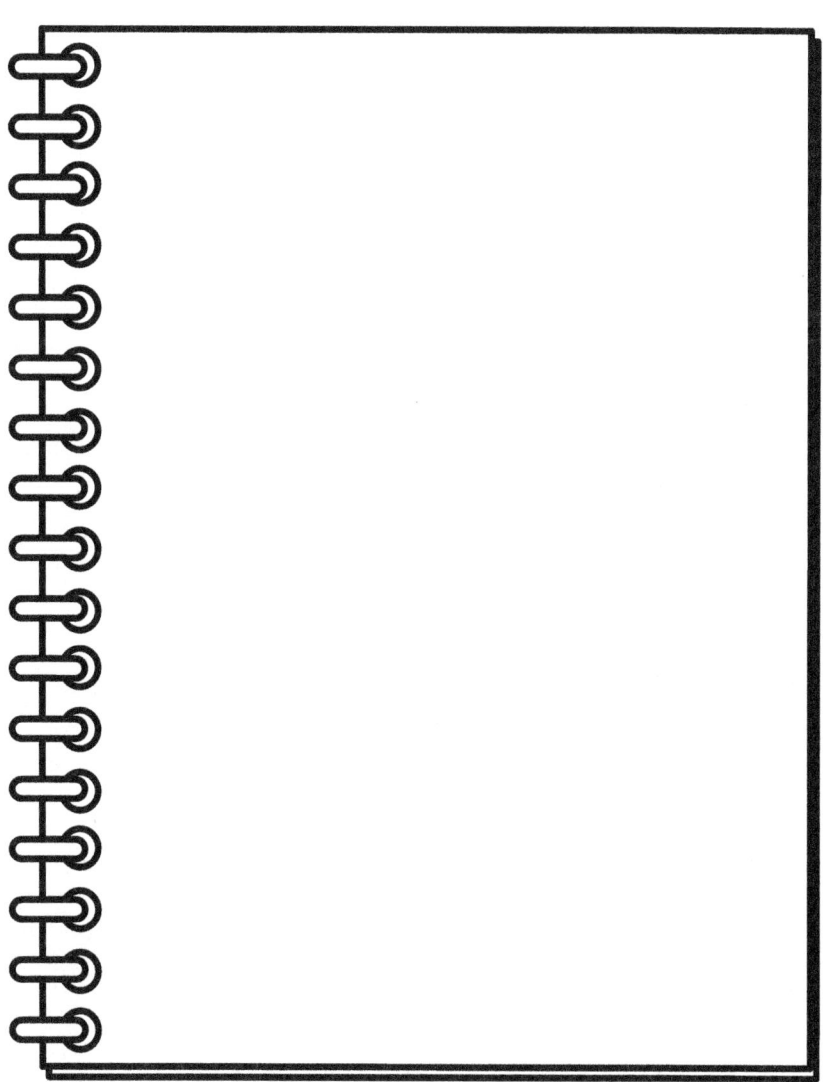

 Church isn't always perfect and sometimes it's not how we want to spend our Sunday mornings. But it is so, so important to keep in mind why we, as Christians, gather together for worship every week.

We don't go to church to earn God's love or have our sins forgiven. We meet together because it's a gift that we can worship God in such beautiful richness and closeness, without a priest or a curtain or the constant sacrifices keeping us stuck in a never-ending loop.

Coming together in worship is such an amazing chance to connect with each other and God that we should make the most of it. In fact, the questions isn't, "Why do we meet together every week?" but rather, "Why *wouldn't* we meet together every week?"

It's such an incredible thing that we get such intimate access to God because of the once-and-for-all sacrifice of Jesus.

Your Notes

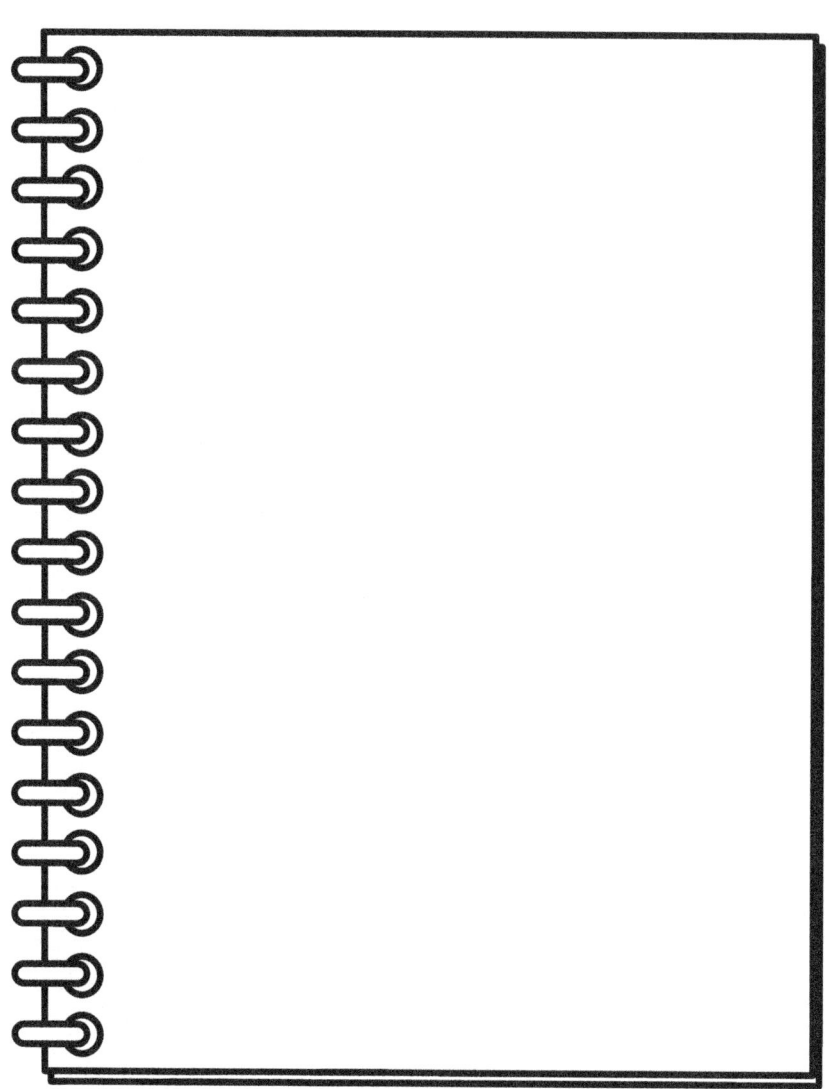

Reflection

But... I Can't be Bothered!

It's Sunday again, and the Church calls my name –
God invites me to worship, to learn and to serve.
A chance to respond, to heal and to grow –
my precious Sunday – a much-needed gift!

God invites me to worship, to learn and to serve –
The community gathered, together in faith.
My precious Sunday – a much-needed gift –
we encourage each other towards love and good deeds!

The community gathered, together in faith –
with all our differences, yet together in worship.
We encourage each other towards love and good deeds –
a reminder once more – I'd be lost if I stopped!

With all our differences, yet together in worship –
a chance to respond, to heal and to grow.
A reminder once more – I'd be lost if I stopped –
it's Sunday again, and the Church calls my name!

M. McKinnell

In Deep

Ideas for Responding in Prayer

Ready to dabble:
Quick and simple prayer ideas

Take a piece of paper, a paper-towel or a tissue. Read Hebrews 10:19-22 again, slowly, and a couple of times through.

As you reflect on the words, gently tear your piece of paper in two, like that temple curtain, and say a prayer of thanks for what God has done.

Going deeper:
Ideas to try if you have more time

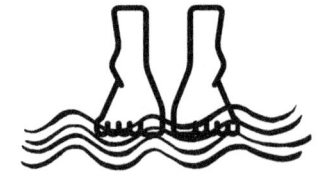

On a square of fabric or on a strong paper towel, draw a large heart in permanent pen. Then, inside the heart, write the word SIN with washable pen. (If you feel able, you could even write one or more specific things for which you want to say sorry to God.)

In a bowl of warm, soapy water, immerse your fabric, and watch as the washable pen dissolves away.

Another way to do this is to write SIN in permanent pen on a whiteboard. Everybody knows you should never use permanent pen on a whiteboard! But... if you go over the letters with a red whiteboard marker, you should find that the whole lot will, mysteriously, wipe away!

Give thanks to God for the joy of his mercy and forgiveness.

Your Notes

Diving right in:
Ideas for personal prayer and journalling

Have you ever tried journalling your way through a Church service?

Take your journal in with you, and as the service goes on, draw or make notes.

Here are some things that you might like to reflect on...

How am I feeling at different points in the service? (You might want to represent this with words, emojis, or colours.)

How do I think the people around me are feeling? What might they be thinking?

What was the preacher/teacher thinking when they prepared today's teaching? What hymns or songs are we singing, and why do I think they were chosen?

What key words or moments of the service jump out at me?

What is something new that I have learned or understand differently after today's service?

Is God speaking to me today? What might God be saying?

Space for Journalling

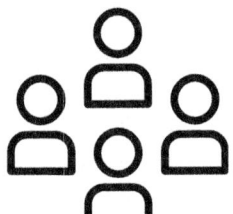

Games and Ideas for Groups

It's SNOWING!!!
Divide your young people into two teams, and give them half of the room each. (A badminton or volleyball net in-between the two sides is ideal.) Then, using plastic balls, balloons or even just scrunched up newspaper, have an indoor snowball fight! Allow the young people three minutes to throw as many 'snowballs' over to the other side as possible, and at the end, the winning team is the one with the least number of snowballs left on their side.

You can use this game to illustrate the circularity of the sacrificial system in the Old Testament, (see Hebrews 10:11). The snowballs keep coming as fast as you throw them out!

Focus on the Positive
It's so easy to get into a whinge-fest when it comes to talking about church. (Grown-ups do this too!) Using a whiteboard or flip chart, or by starting a hashtag on social media, get the young people to list as many *positive* things about church as they can possibly think of. This could include *anything* from the nice atmosphere created by an introit on the organ, to the skills of the drummer in the band, to the quality of the biscuits, to a beautiful stained glass window, to the fact that the toilets are clean... keep going and going and going, until the groups collapses into a daze, or hysteria...

Church at any Cost
In some parts of the world, Christians face persecution, imprisonment or even death for gathering as a church. There are several charities and non-profit organisations that pray for and assist the persecuted church. Find out which organisations have branches or representatives in your area, and see what your group can do to support their work. This might involve fund-raising, praying, or raising awareness.

Ideas for All Age Worship

If the young people have done the 'Focus on the Positive' activity from the Games and Ideas for Groups page, this is an activity that could carry over to All Age Worship.

You could ask people to add to the whiteboard/flip chart as they enter the church, to put ideas onto sticky-notes, or to use the designated hashtag on social media.

Younger members of the congregation might have different ideas to older ones. For example, a pre-schooler might think the toys are the best bit, whereas an adult might want to mention the teaching. Are there some things that all age groups agree with? (Perhaps the importance of biscuits!)

If the young people have been finding out about the persecuted church worldwide, then this is a great theme for an All Age Service. Many of the charities supporting the persecuted church produce resources for worship and prayer.

For a short, interactive prayer activity to include in a service, the ripping-paper activity from 'Ready to Dabble' will work in most contexts.

Bible Study 2
by H. C. Dill

But...
...I don't fit in!

What outfit does God like to see you in?

Colossians 3:1-17

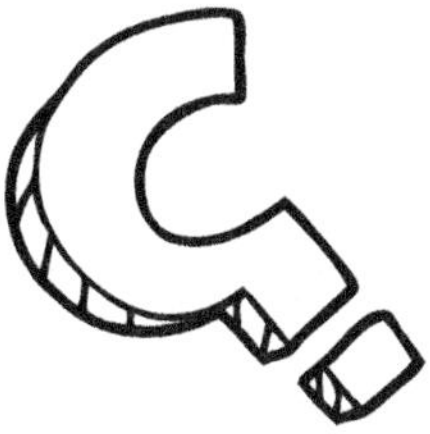

Look again at Colossians 3:10 for the answer.

Have you ever baked a cake?

If you have ever done any baking, you have probably used ingredients like bicarbonate of soda, cream of tartar or baking powder in a recipe. But do you know what these ingredients actually do?

"Yeah, they make the cake rise - right?"

Right. But how do they do that? Most of the time, when we're baking, we don't really know. We add a little spoonful of this and a little spoonful of that just because the recipe tells us to, and even though we don't know how it works... it works!

Colossians 3:1-17 is a bit like a recipe, not for a cake, but for Christian gatherings. It tells us all the ingredients we need when we get together as Christians, plus a few of the things we don't need! More than that, this passage gives us an idea of how these ingredients work in our lives.

Think about a typical worship gathering of your church community, such as a Sunday Morning Service. What 'ingredients' does your gathering have? Do you have singing, teaching, fellowship? Write a list of everything you do when you are together as believers.

What are your favourite things in the list you have made?

Emergency colouring in

Looking at 1 Colossians 3:1-2, what is the overall purpose of gathering for worship?

Your Notes

Verse 3 claims that you are 'dead'! Do you still have a heartbeat? Oh good, then you're not dead - so what is going on in this verse?

The letter to the Colossians was originally written in Greek - a language that has three different words for 'life'. Firstly, there's *Bios*, that's your bodily life - it's where we get the term 'biology' from. Then there's *Psuche*, that's your mind/thoughts and emotions - from which we get the term 'psychology'. But there's also a third kind of life, *Zoe*, which is your eternal life. This is the bit of you that was part of God's plan even before you were born (see Psalm 139:16) and in verse 3 we are promised that our *Zoe* will exist into eternity, protected and loved by Christ in God.

In verses 5-9, what types of behaviour should we work to remove from our lives? Make a list of the things mentioned.

Which of these things relate to your *Bios* and which relate to your *Psuche*?

As a young Christian, which of the behaviours in verses 5-9 do you find easy to put away, and which things are hard to escape or avoid? Why do you think that is?

In verse 5, the letter says that *pleonexian*, (which can be translated as either 'greed' or 'covetousness') is idolatry. Idolatry is the worship of something that is not God. In our modern culture it is easy to worship things that are not God, such as celebrities or money.

Your Notes

What does someone wear when they are being baptised in your church? Do they wear special white clothes, or a christening gown?

In verses 9 and 10 the letter talks about 'putting off' the old self and 'putting on' the new, just like changing into special clothes for a special event.

Turn to Matthew 22:1-14

Who do you think the 'king' is in this parable? What do you notice about the guests in verse 10? Why was one person thrown out in verses 11-12?

This parable seems a bit shocking! Why would somebody be thrown out just for having the wrong clothes? It doesn't seem very 'Christian' does it? But the 'clothes' in this story seem to stand for something else - perhaps baptism. In baptism we accept that we cannot earn a place with God, instead we are given it freely through the death and resurrection of Jesus. (See Ephesians 2:8)

All the putting off and putting on of different things described in Colossians 3:9-14 can seem a bit daunting! But that parable in Matthew reminds us that we don't have to get it right all the time (Matthew 22:10), we just have to be willing to put on a new life - one that is modelled after the image of our creator. (Colossians 3:10)

Have you ever been jealous of someone else's outfit or dress sense? Or have you ever copied a look from a favourite celebrity? In verse 11, what is the effect of 'putting on' the new self that God gives to us?

Your Notes

Verses 12 and 13 give a list of things we should be 'putting on' as followers of Christ. Which of these are you seeing in your life already, and which ones need a bit more work?

 In verse 13, what reason are we given for forgiving and bearing with one another?

There is one ingredient in all this that makes the other ingredients work together. Or perhaps we should say there is one accessory that ties together the whole outfit! It is given in verse 14. What is this special ingredient and what does it do?

Look also at 1 Corinthians 13:1-13. What other things does this special ingredient do? Why do you think it is so effective? (Hint: 1 John 4:8)

Verse 16 mentions singing. In fact, singing is mentioned hundreds of times in the Bible! Singing is good for us in so many ways - it deepens our breathing, reduces stress, makes people feel included... singing has even been shown to boost the human immune system! Even so, church music and singing is often one of the things that Christians complain about the most. Everybody has different ideas about what kind of music is best.

 In verse 16, what should be in our hearts when we are singing our worship to God?

Young people can find it particularly difficult to be heard in discussions about church worship and music. Looking at verse 17, and reflecting on what we have learned throughout this study, what things should or shouldn't we do when we want to speak up on these issues?

Your Notes

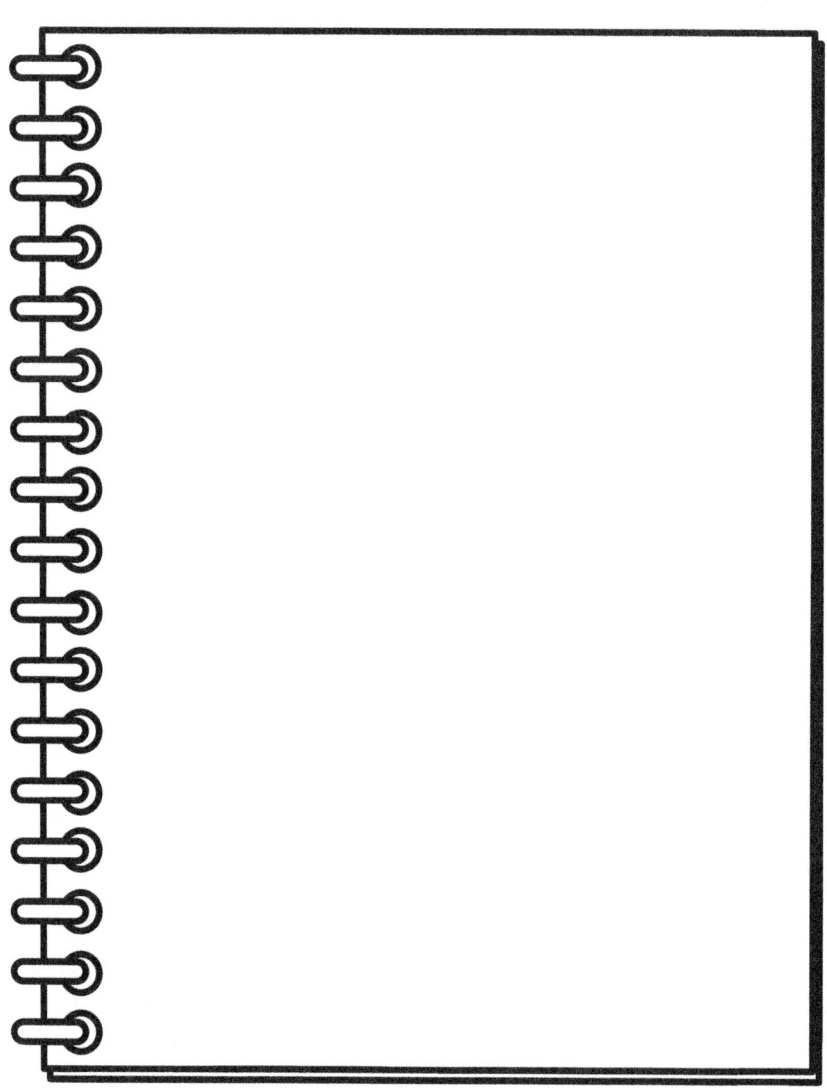

 Sometimes 'church' is a hard thing to understand! There are lots of people there who we might not usually choose to be friends with, and some who do not seem very good at being Christian - including ourselves!

Sometimes the worship gatherings can feel like a disappointment too. We don't always feel like we fit in. People in our church might choose different music from what we like, and have different interests - sometimes it can seem like Christians have nothing in common!

The truth is, all Christians do have something in common - through baptism we have all been 'clothed' with Christ. We might not be making a very perfect job of 'putting on' the new self that comes with being a Christian (verses 12-14), but church is the training ground where we can practice.

Gathering with other Christians helps us with that. Worship gatherings prompt us to re-focus on God (verse 2) and are a place where we can teach, learn and sing to encourage each other in the faith (verse 16). This works, even though we don't all agree on what worship should look and sound like!

The reason it works is that there is a crucial ingredient - just like that raising agent in your cake. The crucial ingredient is **love**, "which binds everything together in perfect harmony" (verse 14).

A harmony is not everybody singing the same note, is it? It is everybody singing different notes that all work together to create a beautiful song. It's important to find your own note when it comes to your church community. Your note might not be quite the same as some of those around you - but that's just fine, (just as long as you don't try to sing it so loud that you drown out everybody else!)

At the end of the day, verse 17 reminds us that church is not about us. It is our way of offering thanksgiving to God, through Christ, who is our *Zoe* (verse 4).

Your Notes

Reflection

But... I Don't Fit In!

When that key ingredient of love is found
within different interests and different tastes –
when kindness, gentleness and patience are at the core,
like a recipe, it always seems to work.

Within different interests and different tastes,
together in harmony, we find companionship –
like a recipe, it always seems to work
when love, crucial love, is binding us as one.

Together in harmony, we find companionship
as part of one family, we are called to peace –
when love, crucial love, is binding us as one,
we can find our place, and God can make things work.

As part of one family, we are called to peace
when kindness, gentleness and patience are at the core –
we can find our place, and God can make things work
when that key ingredient of love is found!

M. McKinnell

In Deep

Ideas for Responding in Prayer

Ready to dabble:
Quick and simple prayer ideas

Write a list of all the things that you do during the week, when you are not at church.

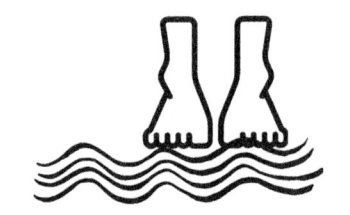

This might include school, work, clubs, hobbies and social activities.

What does it mean to do all of these activities as a person who is 'clothed' in the way Jesus would wish? (Colossians 3:12)

Say a short prayer, asking God to help you to 'put on love' this coming week.

Going deeper:
Ideas to try if you have more time

Gather some wool, string or ribbon in different colours, and assign a colour to each of the virtues listed in Colossians 3:12. Braid the colours together to make a wearable bracelet, which you can put on every day as a reminder that you are 'clothed with Christ.'

Alternatively, using permanent marker or glass-pens, write the virtues around the edge of a hand mirror, or a mirror tile, and place it somewhere that you will see yourself in it each day.

Your Notes

Diving right in:
Ideas for personal prayer and journalling

Make a chart or a calendar for yourself with the virtues down one column and the days of the week across the top.

Every day, try and note down one instance where you have shown compassion, kindness... etc.

	Sunday	Monday	Tuesday
Compassion			
Kindness			
Humility			

At the end of the week, consider which ones you have found easy to do, and which ones have been hard.

What are your goals for growing in godliness?

Space for Journalling

Games and Ideas for Groups

Putting it On
To introduce the theme of this Bible Study, you could set up a relay race where teams have to put on some bulky clothing, complete a set of obstacles, then take the bulky items off again and pass to the next team member, until all the team members have completed the course.
Talk about how it is more difficult to complete the obstacles when you are wearing the 'wrong' clothes!

Role Models
Ask the young people to think about who their role models are for the different areas of their lives. Who's style of dress do they admire, or what about career paths or activism? Do your young people have role models for their Christian life too? In your particular church community, who do they think sets a good example of how to be a Christian? Why have they chosen that particular person?
Conclude by asking the young people to think about whether they are role models, either to younger siblings or to friends at school. Take a sneak peek at 1 Timothy 4:12, which we will look at later in this study guide. Do your young people think that anyone looks to them as an example?

Those Who Serve by Night
Ask the young people to arrive early one week for your weekly worship gathering, and make a list of everything that they see people doing to get set up for the service. Get the young people to stay behind at the end too, and make a list of all the tidying up and putting away. Then, ask them to add everything that might have been done during the week, such as cleaning toilets, arranging flowers, printing service sheets, cleaning crèche toys, purchasing coffee... etc.
Do they have anything on their list that they had never thought about before? Is there anything that they might be able to help with?
Read Psalm 134 and give thanks for all the 'little jobs' that members of your church do, which so often go unnoticed.

Ideas for All Age Worship

And the award goes to…

If the young people have done the 'Those Who Serve by Night' activity based on Psalm 134, why not hold an awards ceremony during or after your service?
Make some fake statuettes, or just print some certificates, dress a couple of young people in tuxedos/ballgowns and have them present awards for 'Toilet Cleaner of The Year', 'Most Frequent Volunteer for Sound Desk' etc.
Try to focus on the behind-the-scenes people, the ones who do all those little jobs that so often get forgotten about.

Songs of the Spirit…

Discussions about music in church are notorious for getting controversial! But do we always focus on the right things? Colossians 3:16 gives us good criteria for selecting the music for our gatherings. Ask the congregation to share which hymns/songs come to mind for the following categories:

- A song that is rich with the message of Christ
- A song that teaches
- A song that admonishes
- A song that is full of wisdom

Are there any surprises? Do old and young give the same answers?

Bible Study 3
by Peter Cross

But...
...I don't get anything out of it!

What is a great way to live?

Romans 12

Look again at Romans 12:18 for the answer.

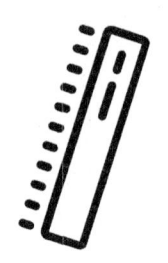

The customer is always right. Right?

That's the way the world works most of the time. And church often feels the same. Church is about what we get out of it, and if it's not working for us then we can find a different church, or just not go...

What do you think makes a good church? Make some notes about what you think worship should look and feel like.

Now look at Romans 12:1-2. What three things do these verses tell us to do?

When we read Romans 12 a new way of seeing church worship opens up for us. Romans is the longest letter written by the Apostle Paul and, to be honest, some of it is pretty dense and hard to wrap our minds around. But the basic thing that Paul is saying is that the old way, the Law of Moses with all the sacrifices and rituals and rules and regulations (remember study 1?), wasn't the full plan of God. Now, through Jesus, we see the real plan unfolding.

When we get to chapter 12, pretty deep into the letter to the Romans, Paul is getting ready to tell his readers what that whole idea means for them. And what he writes has a lot to say to us as well.

Sometimes we think of church a bit like the way we think of a coffee shop. We go to a coffee shop to get something - to have a drink, meet with friends, to sit and study. In a coffee shop, the customer is always right. But what about in church? Should it be the same?

Look at verses 4 and 5. How is being a member of the church different from being a customer in a coffee shop?

Your Notes

Verses 6-8 remind us that we all have something to contribute, a gift to use to build up the church. So, church is not about being a "customer", but about working together.

> What kind of things are you good at?
> Can you think of ways in which you could you use your gifts in the church?

We might need to tread a bit lightly here. It can far too easily move from church not being a place we get something to a place we give something... and then church just becomes a place where we have to regularly go and volunteer or else God's going to be mad at us! That's the furthest thing from what Paul is trying to say here.

Through the whole book of Romans, Paul has been taking apart this idea that you have to do things to earn salvation. That was the "old way". Now, because of Jesus, you don't earn the love of God. In fact, you never really had to! That was never God's intent, but that's what humans chose to make the law into.

The last thing Paul wants us to do is just turn the church into **Law 2.0** where you earn your salvation, but instead of sacrificing sheep and giving some of your crops and showing up in Jerusalem for Passover you volunteer to be a youth helper at holiday club, you go to Sunday School, and you follow loads of rules about what you can and can't do or say. Same old system, new rules.

> Have there been times where you've felt like you had to 'earn' God's love? Was it easy to feel like you were succeeding?
> Look back at verses 1 and 2 of Romans 12. What two things does Paul want us to give to God?

When Paul says "present your bodies as a living sacrifice" remember that he's spent the whole rest of the letter talking about the old sacrificial system of earning salvation. Now, instead of offering up animal sacrifices we ourselves are "living" sacrifices. So, what does that mean?

Your Notes

In verse 1, Paul also says something which is tricky to translate. "This is your spiritual/rational/true and proper act of worship". What does your Bible translation say?

The Greek word is *logikos,* and if you see the English word *logic* in there, you'd be exactly right. The word *logikos* does mean something like what we may think of as *logical*.

So, the fact that this word is sometimes translated as *spiritual* may seem sort of odd at first, but in the ancient world *logic* was about your mind and your soul together. The ancients believed that using your mind for reasoning things out was tapping into your spiritual side, as opposed to just listening to the urges of your body. (So, "stomach empty eat food now!" is a bodily thought, not a *logikos* type of thought...make sense?)

So, what Paul is saying is "Don't be a mindless, rule-following drone". The Christian faith is not about blindly following rules. It is a *logikos* act of worship.

Have you ever felt like church is just about rules? What are some of your least favourite 'rules' you've been told in church?

Verse 2 clears it up for us even more: "...be transformed by the renewing of your mind."

You see, church isn't about getting something, but it's also not just about giving something either. It's about transformation. The word here is where we get the English word *metamorphosis* and it's something that is continuous and ongoing. This transformation is also much bigger than just ourselves... and this is where it gets really cool! While we are being transformed, and we're together with other Christians who are being transformed, then together we can begin to transform the whole world!

Can you think of some parts of our world that need transformation the most?

Your Notes

Look at verses 9-21. Paul is giving a picture here of what our transformed selves, churches and world should look like! It's a pretty amazing picture isn't it?

Our transformation doesn't stop with us and our own lives. It then works together with people around us who are also going through the same *metamorphosis* in order to change the pattern of that world and make a new one. A pattern that is centred on love and welcome and humility... basically all the things Paul goes on about in the rest of the chapter!

Make a list of all the good things Paul mentions in verses 9-21 that come out of a transformed life. Which ones do you feel you are seeing in your life already, and with which ones could you use a little help?

So, maybe your church is boring... *really* boring... zzzzzzzz.....

But church isn't about what you get out of it, and it's also not just a place to volunteer!

Romans 12 tells us that church is so much more than that. And, once we're clued into that, we can see how each and every one of us has a part to play. We each have something that makes us uniquely us. And the transformation process is partly about unlocking those things that make you *you,* because God loves you exactly how you are.

That *you* is going to be the best at making this world a transformed place. Church can help us with unlocking that special role we each have. What a really exciting thing to be part of!

Your Notes

Reflection

But... I Don't get Anything Out of It!

It's no longer a world of restrictions and rules,
we need unlocking, our unique roles revealed.
When every thought, word and deed is worship to God –
we're renewed and transformed, as God's precious kin!

We need unlocking, our unique roles revealed,
as Christ is complete when our gifts are combined.
We're renewed and transformed, as God's precious kin –
the church shines brightly with welcome and love!

As Christ is complete when our gifts are combined,
we each have our part to play in church life.
The church shines brightly with welcome and love –
our appreciation of worship grows stronger each day!

We each have our part to play in church life,
when every thought, word and deed is worship to God.
Our appreciation of worship grows stronger each day –
it's no longer a world of restrictions and rules!

M. McKinnell

In Deep

Ideas for Responding in Prayer

Ready to dabble:
Quick and simple prayer ideas

Using an ink-pad, make a copy of your fingerprint on a piece of paper.

Each person's fingerprint is totally unique. Even identical twins do not have the same!

Spend some time looking at your fingerprint and thanking God for the things that make you totally unique.

You could even turn your fingerprint into a finger-labarynth for prayer! The easiest way to do this is to take a photograph of the print on your phone, and zoom in so that it is large enough for you to follow the pattern with your eyes or the point of a pencil.

Going deeper:
Ideas to try if you have more time

Looking back at Study 2, did you identify any ways in which you can serve your church community?

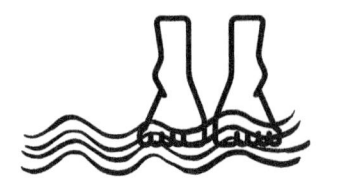

Do you think that taking an active part has helped you to grow in your Christian life, or has made you feel any different about coming to church?

Are there any new ways that you could serve, or new areas of ministry that you would like to develop in your church?

Your Notes

Diving right in:
Ideas for personal prayer and journalling

In Romans 12:2 Paul talks about transformation.

In what ways do you think being part of a church has transformed you?

Are there any areas of your life which still need transformation?

Imagine yourself and what you will be like in five or ten years time.

How old will you be? What will you be doing?

Most importantly, what will your Christian life look like?

In what ways do you think being a church-goer will make a difference to the kind of person you become?

Space for Journalling

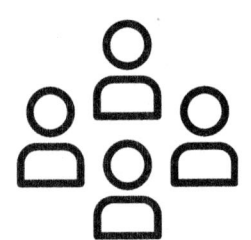

Games and Ideas for Groups

It Takes All Sorts...
This game involves a bit of preparation, and you need to know your young people fairly well, but it is a good way to illustrate the point that everyone is important and has something to give.
Design a scavenger hunt that can only be completed by using the skills of everyone in the team. For example, if you know that one of your young people speaks a foreign language, one of the items might be to write the word 'hello' in that language. Or, if you have a young person who is particularly tall, ask the team to 'collect a leaf that is growing more than 2 metres off the ground' and so on...
At the end, tell the young people that you designed the hunt to use everybody's skills. How well do they think they did? Did everybody in their team get a chance to participate?

What Do Others See?
Tape a piece of paper to the back of each person, and give out felt-tip pens. For an allotted time period, ask the young people to go around and write down compliments on each other's backs. They must be specific *to that person*, i.e., you're good at singing/listening/organising... and not too vague, i.e., you're nice...
At the end of the time, the young people can remove their own sheet and read what others have written. Is there anything there that surprises them, or that they didn't think other people had noticed?

See, I am Doing a New Thing...
The young people have already thought about how they could fit in to the existing life of your church, but what about starting something new? Is there a new avenue of outreach, or a new type of worship service that your young people want to try? Why not put together a proposal for your church leadership team, and see what they think?

Ideas for All Age Worship

Everyone in the church contributes something, even if they don't realise it.

Give each member of the congregation a paper hand-shape, or ask them to draw round their own hand on paper. On each finger they should write one thing that they bring, give or do to serve in the church. This should include things in the present and in the past, as some people will have retired after many years of faithful duty. The list might include things like donating money, leading worship, making coffee, pastoral care, singing in the choir... or simply being present! After all, Church wouldn't be the same without a few bouncing toddlers keeping everyone amused.

Once all the hands have been completed and cut out, they can be used to make a display in the shape of a mural or Pentecost fire.

Using the fingerprint prayer idea from 'Ready to Dabble', you could lead into a time of prayer, giving thanks for the unique contribution that everybody makes.

Bible Study 4

by H. C. Dill

But...
...Church is *Boring!*

Why was the Apostle Paul pumping iron?

1 Timothy 4:6-16

Look again at 1 Timothy 4:8 for the answer.

Paul was getting on a bit. He was not a young man anymore. So, he adopted Timothy as his 'spiritual child' (see 1 Timothy 1:2) - someone who could lead the church when Paul was no longer around.

In 1 Timothy we find a whole letter-full of advice from the Apostle Paul to his young protégé on how to lead the church at Ephesus. It's worth reading the whole letter, but we will look specifically at chapter 4:6-16.

In verses 6-8 Paul talks about 'training' in godliness. The Greek word is *gymnaze* - from which we get the English word *gymnasium*.

Have you ever tried sticking to an exercise plan at home instead of at the gym? Is it easier or harder to stick to a plan and push yourself when you are working out by yourself?

I don't know about you, but I definitely find it easier to work out in an environment that is dedicated to the task! And I definitely put more effort into training when I'm training with friends or in a fitness class.

It can help us to think about church this way too. Yes, we can worship, pray and read our Bibles at home, on the bus...or anywhere! But it's much easier to make progress and stay motivated when we work together with others who share our goals.

In verses 7 and 8, what does Paul say we are we training for?

When we train in the gym, we are not only strong in the gym! The strength we gain goes home with us.

The godliness that Paul speaks about in verses 7 and 8 is like this too. Godliness is not just learned *at* church *for* church, but about being worshipful in every area of our lives.

Your Notes

The 'silly myths' mentioned in verse 7 refers back to what people have been doing in verses 1-5. Have you ever met a Christian who tries to make being a Christian into a million-and-one finicky rules? See Colossians 2:2-23 for some more of what Paul has to say about that.

In verse 8, what two time periods does Paul give, when godliness will be of some value? Does this suprise you?

Can you think of some ways in which this might be true? (Hint: Revelation 3:20-21.)

Verse 9 contains a little 'saying' that Paul uses *only* in the letters to Timothy and Titus! There a 5 occurrences of this 'saying' - can you find the others?*

Paul uses his 'saying' when he wants to emphasise a particular point. What do you think is the point he is emphasising here? (Verse 10)

Who is saved in verse 10? It's a tricky question, isn't it? This phrase (and a similar one in Titus 2:11-12) seems to suggest that all people are saved, whether they believe in God or not!

However, in many other places the New Testament seems to say the direct opposite, (Romans 10:9; John 3:16; 1 John 5:12). Theologians have argued about this for centuries, but it is most likely to mean simply that everyone has the *potential* to be saved, but we can be *sure* of those who believe. Importantly, we should not forget that at the end of the day, it is up to God, not us! (2 Timothy 1:9; Ephesians 2:8-9)

How would you summarise what Timothy should teach? (Verse 11)

*1 Timothy 1:15; 1 Timothy 3:1; 2 Timothy 2:11; Titus 3:8

Your Notes

In verse 12, what reason does Paul suggest for people not listening to Timothy's teaching?

How does Paul advise Timothy should overcome this?

Have you ever heard the phrase 'actions speak louder than words'? Paul is saying that, even though he is young, Timothy can teach the believers through his way of life as well as through his words.

Timothy was a young man, but looking at verses 13-14, what role do you think he had in the church?

What kind of role(s) do young people have in your church? Do you think it is OK to take on a position of responsibility, even if you are still learning and growing? (Verse 15)

In verse 16, what will be the benefit of Timothy staying true to his calling?

If church is boring, then something is not right!

All people, including young people, have an important role in the church, helping everyone to train in godliness.

Church may be difficult sometimes, since all believers are works-in-progress (verse 15). But your presence has as much to contribute to other people's growth as it does to your own (verse 10).

If you are finding church boring, then maybe you have not yet found the right way to work out your own calling or vocation. You should speak to your church leadership about this (verse 14), and ask them to help you find ways to serve the church community.

Some churches won't be used to having young people stepping up into leadership and service. But remember verse 12! If your words seem to go unheard, let your actions teach and serve the believers instead!

Your Notes

Reflection

But... Church is *Boring!*

Don't silence me, brother, just cause I'm young –
It would be all too easy to forget church, and God.
I, too, am God's child, and a work-in-progress –
if our church life is boring, then somethings not right!

It would be all too easy to forget church, and God –
I need your encouragement, it's the best motivation.
If our church life is boring, then somethings not right –
as I learn from you and, yes, you learn from me!

I need your encouragement, it's the best motivation –
as together we serve, through both word and action.
As I learn from you and, yes, you learn from me –
we are all, young and old, commissioned by God!

As together we serve, through both word and action –
I, too, am God's child, and a work-in-progress.
We are all, young and old, commissioned by God –
don't silence me, sister, just cause I'm young!

M. McKinnell

In Deep

Ideas for Responding in Prayer

Ready to dabble:
Quick and simple prayer ideas

We have thought a lot about what we bring to the church, but in 1 Timothy 4:8 we are reminded that our 'training' together is something we take away with us into every area of our lives.

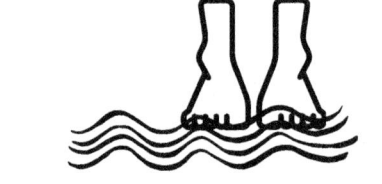

Write down as many things as you can think of that you 'take away' from attending church, and put them into a (clean!) take-away box from your local restaurant.

You may want to keep this going over several weeks, adding in things that you have learned or been encouraged by.

Going deeper:
Ideas to try if you have more time

D. L. Moody once famously illustrated the importance of church attendance by taking a hot coal out of the fire, and showing how quickly it went cold when left alone on the hearth.

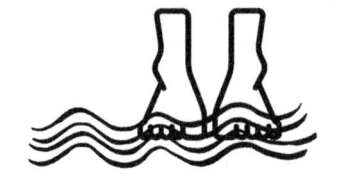

Most people don't have a coal fire anymore, but try taking a bowl of hot water, a small cup and two thermometers. Scoop a small amount of the hot water from the bowl into the cup, place a thermometer in each, and watch how much more quickly the temperature goes down for the water in the cup. As you do so, ask God to help you stay faithful and committed to your church community, even when it gets a little bit... *boring*!

Your Notes

Diving right in:
Ideas for personal prayer and journalling

Take a look at The Parable of the Sower in Matthew 13:3-9.

We often take the different types of soil to be different types of people, but parables can often be understood in more than one way.

What if the different types of soil referred to different areas of your life? In what places is the Word of God able to grow strongly and produce fruit, and in what places does it get choked by weeds or scorched and withered?

Try looking at Matthew 13:18-23 for some ideas. Are there areas of your life where you are too overwhelmed with worry to make space for God, or where your faith is persecuted?

Looking back over the four studies as a whole, in what ways can being part of a church help you overcome the challenges of the Christian life?

Have your thoughts and feelings about church changed at all?

Have you been able to develop or change your role in the church?

Would you want to change your answers to any of the questions in the 'Prepare' section, or in the early studies in this book?

Space for Journalling

Games and Ideas for groups

Circuit Training

Divide the young people into two or more teams, and challenge them to devise a *challenging* circuit-training or obstacle course that the other team(s) must complete. It should be designed to test both fitness and endurance.

In all likelihood, the teams will come up with something particularly gruelling for the others to complete. But THEN, change the rules. The teams must now complete their OWN circuit!

Sit back and smugly enjoy a beverage, while they suffer and get out of breath. Then lead into a discussion about how our focus should be on our *own* training, and not on making up rules for other people (1 Timothy 4:16).

Dear...

Looking back over the four studies as a whole, ask the young people to contribute to a list of all the things that they have learned. Then, mimicking the style of the Apostle Paul, get them to write an 'Epistle' (i.e., a letter) to an imaginary young person who is not attending church, or who is complaining that church is *boring*. What advice would they give? The young people might want to look at the beginning and ending of some of the other Epistles to get an idea of how they usually start and finish.

Lights, Cameras, Action...

Challenge the young people to make a promo video for your church, or a fly-on-the-wall documentary. They can include everything they have learned about how the church operates week-to-week, including all the ministries and activities that go on behind the scenes. They may want to include interviews with key members of the church. Make sure that the young people have the appropriate permission to film anyone that is included in their video, and remind them to be especially sensitive about filming during worship.

Ideas for All Age Worship

If young people have made a video about your church, then All Age Worship might be a good place to share this with the wider congregation.

Likewise, the young people may want to share some or all of their 'Epistle', if they have written one. You could even sneak it into the service as one of the Scripture readings, giving it a fake-but-convincing sounding reference (i.e., 1 Timothy 7:1-8) to see if anyone notices!

A simpler idea that requires little preparation is the 'take-away' box from the 'Ready to Dabble' section. You could ask all members of the congregation to jot down one thing that they will 'take-away' from the service that day. Put them all in the take-away box and mix them up. Then, as everyone is leaving they should select somebody else's contribution and take it away with them.

Bonus Content!

by H. C. Dill

But...
...How do we welcome young people?

A study for the wider church family

Where do you find the one and the many?

1 Corinthians 12

Look again at 1 Corinthians 12:20 for the answer.

Sometimes, as adults, we struggle to help young people embed themselves within church life. Adult members tend to have their place and be confident in their allotted tasks, and it can be hard to change the way things are done, or delegate a task to someone who might not complete it to the same polished standard.

Many churches do not even realise that they are leaving their young people out. It is too easy to make assumptions about how committed or capable young people are - assumptions that may not be correct!

Read 1 Corinthians 12 all the way through, then focus in on verses 4-6. What do you think the problem at the church in Corinth might have been?

Paul affirms that we all have spiritual gifts. In verse 7, for what purpose are these gifts given to us?

Look at verses 8-10, and also at verse 28. Which gifts have you observed, or do you expect to find, among young people?

Read verse 13. Your church may not have many Jews, Greeks or slaves in it! How would you re-write this verse to reflect your modern context?

Looking at verses 15 and 18, who decides which members are part of the body, and where in the body each member should fit?

Paul likens the church to a human body in all ways except one - in the church body the 'weak and the dishonourable' are our best features!

How well do we do in the modern-day church at giving pride of place to those whom society treats as 'weak' or 'dishonoured'?

Your Notes

Q In verses 24-25, what is the purpose of turning the heirarchy of honour and dishonour on its head?

Who, in your church, tends to be thought of as the most important person, or group of people?

In verses 28-31, Paul presents the various gifts like a ladder, with apostles at the top.

The word 'apostle' literally means 'the one who is sent out' - like an emissary or messenger.

Q By this measure, who is the most important person, or group of people, in your church?

Read on a little way in 1 Corinthians 13, focussing on verses 4-5. Is there anything that you resolve to do differently, in order to show love and honour to the young people in your church community?

A **1 Corinthians 12 calls for a radically different way of evaluating who and what is important in a church.** It's a way of being that stands entirely at odds with our consumerist, celebrity-driven culture.

But, importantly, it *is* possible, especially when love is at the core of everything that we do.

Young people are indispensable, both as learners *and teachers* in the church. Not only that, but outside of the church, in work or education, they are apostles, just like the rest of us.

Your Notes

Reflection

But... how do we welcome young people?

We're not leaving the young folk out, are we,
when we're comfortable in our established roles?
We share in joys and sorrows as they find their way –
remember, we were once young and willing learners too.

When we're comfortable in our established roles,
challenged by youthly eagerness to serve.
Remember, we were once young, and willing learners too –
yet we struggle to help them embrace church life.

Challenged by youthly eagerness to serve,
we must open our hearts to what they teach us.
Yet we struggle to help them embrace church life –
still, we're united as apostles, young and old, together.

We must open our hearts to what they teach us,
we share in joys and sorrows as they find their way.
Still, we're united as apostles, young and old, together –
we're not leaving the young folk out, are we?

M. McKinnell

About the Authors

H. C. Dill
Henna is a freelance writer and Christian youth worker. She lives in Aberdeenshire, Scotland with her husband and two children. Dill holds both a First Class Honours Degree and a Masters-by-Research in Theology from the University of Aberdeen. She has many years of experience in children and youth ministry, working with groups of all shapes and sizes, across different denominations.

To contact H. C. Dill, and to be kept up-to-date on future publications in this series, please visit the author's social media pages on Facebook (H.C.DillWrite) or Instagram (@h.c.dill.write).

Mary McKinnell
Mary has an interest in Ignatian Spirituality and much of her writing comes out of using spiritual practices from this tradition. She draws on Scripture and on a wide variety of personal and church related experiences for inspiration. Mary has many years' experience working for the church as a communications mission officer, helping others to communicate Christ's love to their local community. She is also a trained spiritual director and enjoys this ministry, listening to others and supporting them in their relationship with God.
Mary also enjoys writing and leading worship services, reflective days and residential retreats, to help people of all ages to spend time with God.

You can view more of Mary's work or contact her via her blog: searchingforunderstanding.com

About the Authors

Peter Cross
Peter is a Church Ministries worker in Aberdeenshire, Scotland. He is originally from New Mexico, USA, and holds degrees in Theology and Biblical Studies. Peter has over 12 years of experience in youth work in both America and Scotland. He is particularly passionate about faith and issues of social justice. In his spare time, Peter enjoys spending time with his wife, Katie, his dog, Merlin, and sampling various brands of hot sauce.

Donna Kriel
Donna is originally from Ayrshire in Scotland, and came to faith while in her second year at the University of Aberdeen. Donna holds a degree in Spacial Planning, but felt called to Youth Ministry after graduating, and has since devoted more than ten years to teaching and mentoring young people in the Christian faith.
Donna lives in Aberdeen with her husband and two wee boys, and the whole family enjoys camping, cycling and adventures.

Still hungry?

Why not check out our website?

www.butbiblestudy.com

There, you can:

- Check out other titles in the But... series
- Find out more about the authors
- Submit your own suggestions for future titles

We look forward to seeing you there!

Printed in Great Britain
by Amazon